CURLY-COATED RL┌╌┴╌╌┴╌┘╌┘╌┘

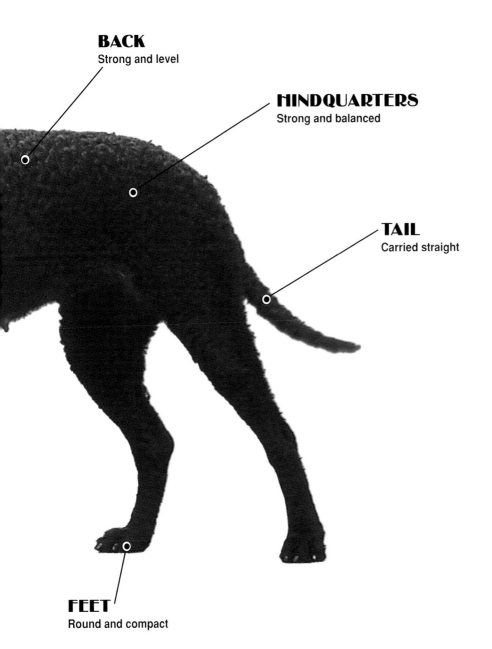

BACK
Strong and level

HINDQUARTERS
Strong and balanced

TAIL
Carried straight

FEET
Round and compact

Title page: Curly-Coated Retriever owned by authors Gary and Mary Meek

Photographers: Cindy Caldwell, Stephanie Doerr, Isabelle Francais, Cathy Lewandowski, Gary Meek, Mary Meek, Photos Today, Ross Round, Caroline Stewart, Karen Van Hoy

Distributed in the UNITED STATES to the Pet Trade by T.F.H. Publications, Inc., 1 TFH Plaza, Neptune City, NJ 07753; on the Internet at www.tfh.com; in CANADA by Rolf C. Hagen Inc., 3225 Sartelon St., Montreal, Quebec H4R 1E8; Pet Trade by H & L Pet Supplies Inc., 27 Kingston Crescent, Kitchener, Ontario N2B 2T6; in ENGLAND by T.F.H. Publications, PO Box 74, Havant PO9 5TT; in AUSTRALIA AND THE SOUTH PACIFIC by T.F.H. (Australia), Pty. Ltd., Box 149, Brookvale 2100 N.S.W., Australia; in NEW ZEALAND by Brooklands Aquarium Ltd., 5 McGiven Drive, New Plymouth, RD1 New Zealand; in SOUTH AFRICA by Rolf C. Hagen S.A. (PTY.) LTD., P.O. Box 201199, Durban North 4016, South Africa; in JAPAN by T.F.H. Publications, Japan—Jiro Tsuda, 10-12-3 Ohjidai, Sakura, Chiba 285, Japan. Published by T.F.H. Publications, Inc.
MANUFACTURED IN THE
UNITED STATES OF AMERICA
BY T.F.H. PUBLICATIONS, INC.

CURLY-COATED RETRIEVER

A COMPLETE AND RELIABLE HANDBOOK

Gary and Mary Meek

RX-119

CONTENTS

ORIGIN OF THE CURLY-COATED RETRIEVER

In England during the mid-1800s, the dog used by gamekeepers and poachers alike to retrieve downed birds was the Curly-Coated Retriever. The Curly was known as the ultimate "meat dog," as his intelligence, determination, and nose made him invaluable in finding downed birds. The tight curls of his coat were impervious to weather and dense, rough field conditions.

One of the first questions people ask when they see a Curly is, "Where did they come from?" The Curly as we know it today was developed in England. Curly Water Dogs have been in use since the early 1800s. According to Phillip Ashburton, there was indisputable evidence that in Norfolk and Lincolnshire, where Robin Hood lived, Curlies existed around 1490.

The Water Dog was not like the Water Spaniel. He was considerably larger in size, proportion, and substance. His muzzle was short, the ears of moderate length, and the coat was curled and shaggy all over. The tail was short and somewhat erect, and the color was usually black and white.

In *British Quadrupeds* (1837), Thomas Bell wrote, "The peculiar qualities and propensities of this dog, its exquisite sense of smell, its sagacity, strength and aquatic habits, have rendered it a most useful and important servant to a particular class of persons of the North of England and Scotland who live principally by shooting water fowl, in the retrieving of which these dogs exhibit the highest degree of docility and hardihood."

In the *Sportsman's Repository* of 1820, John Scott

Sportsmen love to work with Curlies. This is Decke, owned by Julia Smith, waiting to begin the hunt.

says about Water Dogs, "The original Water Dog of the opposite continent being long since adopted in this country and in some of the maritime districts is still preserved in a state of purity, but the breed is more generally intermixed with the Water Spaniel and Newfoundland dog."

As there were no breeding records kept before the mid-1800s, several crosses with this Curly Water Dog may have influenced the Curly of today. The St. Johns Newfoundland, the Tweed Spaniel, the Irish Water Spaniel, and the Poodle all may have added some degree of influence to the final form that the Curly took by 1860.

The Curly-Coated Retriever was first shown in England in 1860 in the Retriever Class and has changed little in appearance since that time. The Curly was the first retriever shown in England and he was probably the first of the retrieving breeds developed there. By the late 1800s, the Labrador and the Flat-Coated Retriever seemed to be seen in larger numbers at the shows.

The popularity of the Curly has ebbed and flowed

throughout its history with no single reason for it. The breed admirers have always appreciated the dog's beauty and intelligence. Its detractors, often those who have never worked with a Curly, condemned them for having a hard mouth. Those of us who hunt behind these wonderful dogs will attest to the fact that Curlies do not, overall, have a hard mouth.

It has also been said that the Curly's coat is hard to care for in the field. This is false. His crisp, dense curls repel water, burrs, and damage from rough cover, and they often come out of the field unscarred while other retrievers lose coat and skin and attract burrs.

The tightly curled coat of the Curly repels water, burrs, and prevents damage that other sporting dogs with softer, thinner coats cannot escape.

THE CURLY-COATED RETRIEVER IN ENGLAND

As there were no records of breeding kept before the late 1800s, we have little knowledge of the people who developed the modern-day Curly. It is believed that there were crosses with other breeds of Water Dogs until this time. The Kennel Club then began to keep records, and we can see the development of this breed by those who loved it most.

If you were to follow the pedigrees of your Curlies back to the early 1900s, you would find that the most predominate prefixes of that time were Penworthan, Preston, Knysna, Notlaw, and Coombehurst.

Opposite: It has been said that Curlies have a hard mouth. On the contrary, Curlies are soft-mouthed and regularly handle game with care.

The First World War saw a dramatic drop in the Curly population, mostly because of the lack of food. A few people, however, helped to keep the breed alive even in those very rough times. In the 1930s, we see the beginnings of the Darelyn and Snaphill Kennels, but again England was thrust into another war. Dogs were shipped to potentially safe places to await the end of the war, yet the breed almost died out for the second time in 30 years.

In the 1940s, there was a resurgence of the Darelyn stock, with Delilah of Darelyn and Dru of Darelyn. These dogs were the beginning of the present-day Darelyn stock. Akrow was another important breeding prefix that was responsible for the Sarona and Turkamann stock that rose to importance in the 1950s.

At this point, we begin to see the following prefixes in our pedigrees: Banworth, Harkaway, Grinkle, Trambitops, and Burtoncurl. Each began to dominate the English pedigrees in the 1950s and 1960s, along with Darelyn, Siccawei, Renniston, and Charcol.

During this time, there was some very active breeding being done, and the number of Curlies in England grew. We began to see the importation of Curlies to

The history of Curly-Coated Retrievers is filled with stories of hunting throughout the world. These two probably hope to follow the example set by their ancestors.

Australia, Scandinavia, and the US. The growth of the breed continued into the '70s and '80s with the Harkaway, Darelyn, Banworth, Rosthwaite, Pentar, Saxonholme and Gladrags, Grenowood, Tangules, and Ladybrow prefixes coming to the forefront.

Ch. Darelyn Rifleman began his historic show career in the 1980s, with Best in Show wins against dog entries of 16,315 and 23,627 at England's biggest shows. He became an important producer and his offspring are in every pedigree throughout England, Europe, and Australia, and he now has new imports even in the US.

Today, Darelyn is the dominant prefix found worldwide. Brenal, Groomswood, and Gladrags are also making their mark on the Curly today in England and all over the world. Many breeders, using these and other prefixes, have developed the modern Curly and have influenced the development of the breed worldwide. Hopefully, the best is yet to come.

THE CURLY IN AUSTRALIA

Records indicate that the Curly was an established breed in Australia by 1880. The first recorded information goes back to the early 1800s and there is reason to believe that the Curly existed in Australia even before then. The modern-day Curly in Australia and New Zealand was developed from Native Australian, New Zealander, and English imports.

In *Dogs in Australia* (1897), by Walter Bielby, Martins Ravensdown Ben was a success at the Victoria Show. T. Maude's Lucifer (UK import) was an excellent specimen, but there were no bitches with whom to breed. B. & F. Cotton imported a pair, Nelson Prince and Nelson Beauty (his daughter), and they were bred to produce Black Prince.

Olaf Michelson of Victoria bred under the name Tablik and his stock was the foundation for most of Australia's Curlies. He was actively showing until the 1950s.

In New South Wales, Noel Janson (Crescent) and Don Tatterson (Glenholden) were prominent breeders in the '30s, '40s, and '50s.

Importation from England slowed after the war, but those that were brought in are prominent in today's pedigrees. In the '50s, Darelyn Aristocrat, Irishit Straight Line, and Prince of Knocksginan were imported. The '60s saw the importing of Sarona Simon, Banworth Athene, and Pegasus. Lectim Kennels imported Banworth Simon, and possibly 80-90 percent of today's Curlies carry his bloodlines in Australia.

The '70s marked the beginning of the importation of New Zealand Curlies. The first was Ch. Waitoki Tuhora, QC. Many dogs today carry her bloodlines. Aust. Ch. Mahemanee Riwi, QC, a liver male, sired many top-producing sires and dams.

Australia began exporting Curlies to America during the '70s, as well as to Germany, New Guinea, and New Zealand. They are now becoming a part of breed history outside of Australia.

The Australians prize their Curlies as hunting dogs because they are sturdy enough to easily retrieve birds as large as swans. They have even been used to hunt kangaroo. It takes a brave, intelligent, and agile dog to take on a kangaroo and come out alive.

NEW ZEALAND CURLIES

In New Zealand, the Curly is the most popular hunting retriever. Size varies more there and some lines look almost like American Water Spaniels. This is the only country where the smaller version of the Curly seems to exist. The smaller Curly has been dubbed the "Murray River Curly" because it is found along the Murray River and is a most popular duck

Curlies are utilized in New Zealand as well as in America for their talents in the water and field.

Opposite: These two buddies demonstrate the Curly's talent for retrieving.

dog. It is unregistered but many think it should be its own breed. Pat Baker of Waitoki Kennels is the source of most Curlies imported into Australia and the US.

The Curlies in New Zealand are prized for their field and aquatic ability, and although beauty has its place, brains and physical ability take precedence. Field trialing takes up the time between hunting seasons.

CURLIES IN AMERICA

Curlies were initially introduced in this country in 1907. Knysma Conjurer was the first Curly registered with the AKC Stud Book in 1924. During the 1920s and 1930s, Curlies were very popular as gundogs because of their legendary adaptability to various hunting situations. Many people today remember having a Curly in the family as a child. By the 1950s, most of the hunting kennels had begun to breed rapidly maturing and flashier retrievers, and many owners of Curlies were unable to replace their old hunting companions.

In 1966, Dale Detweiler imported Ch. Siccawei Black Rod from England, and the dog became the foundation of our present day American Curlies. Many old AKC judges remember "Limey" in the show ring, as well as many hunters who had the pleasure of hunting behind him in the field. Dale continued to import and promote the Curly under the kennel name Windpatch. He is considered by many as the father of the modern-day American Curly.

Besides Dale Detweiler's Windpatch Curlies, the US has seen the breed develop under such kennel names as Karakul, Summerwind, Sevenraven, Wits End, Charwin, Ptarmigan, El Mack, Mayhem, and Aarowag. More enthusiasts join these veteran breeders in their quest to continually improve this wonderful breed.

The Curly-Coated Retriever Club of America was chartered in 1979. The club publishes a newsletter, has a rescue program, holds a National Specialty and Field Day each year, and is now an AKC-licensed club. Breeders can be located through a directory that can be sent to all that request information on the Curly.

Although the Curly-Coated Retriever is still rare in the US, reputable breeders can be found across the country who are breeding physically sound dogs with excellent hunting abilities that make fine show dogs and family companions.

CHARACTERISTICS OF THE CURLY-COATED RETRIEVER

If you are looking for a unique retriever, then the Curly may be of interest to you. His short, tight, crisp black or liver coat is relatively maintenance free and impervious to any weather or cover he may encounter as your hunting companion.

The Curly is a strongly built, intelligent, loyal, inde-

His hardy personality and tough coat make the Curly an excellent companion for most any hunter.

pendent, and gentle dog with a unique sense of humor. Their size ranges from 21 inches and 50 pounds to over 27 inches and over 90 pounds. The standard recommends 25-27 inches for males and 23-25 inches for females. A Curly should carry size and bone without losing elegance or agility.

Because the Curly is so intelligent, he is active in body and mind. Although easily trained, he can be somewhat stubborn and self-willed. Socializing your puppy to the sights and sounds of the world outside of his own home, yard, family, and friends is very important. A Curly that is taught manners and obedience from puppyhood on and exposed to the world around him will grow up to be a charming companion.

Since Curlies learn quickly and remember what they learn, constant repetition of a training exercise will tend to bore him. Training is most successful when varied and of short duration. Curlies seldom need more than a harsh word when a correction is in order.

Because of his size and energy level, a Curly needs a fenced yard and an active family that is willing to spend ample time with him on a daily basis. As with all retrievers, the Curly needs plenty of exercise or he will find things to do on his own. Although he has a great imagination, his antics will not always be acceptable to you, but he will always do it with a smile! Something once learned or discovered is never forgotten by a Curly, so opening doors, escaping from crates, opening gates, etc., means that his humans must change the situation or fortify things to keep their Curly from repeating his newly learned tricks.

The Curly is an excellent companion for children; adult Curlies are instinctively gentle with small ones. He is not usually aggressive and will accept other animals within his domain. Because the Curly is such a sociable animal, he does best while living within the family home and not as a kennel or yard dog.

Curlies are not usually barkers, but they will bark a warning when someone or something is around. Determined and loyal, a Curly will stand his ground, if necessary, between his family and possible danger. From his first day with you, a Curly puppy should be taught the rules of the house. A puppy socialization and beginning obedience class is not only necessary, but will help give you, the owner, the proper tools to train a Curly that is easy to live with both at and away from home.

Today, Curlies are found working in the field as well as the marshlands of America. He is said to be a "meat hunter's dog," which means that he is an independent hunter, needing little direction to locate and retrieve game. His persistence and ability to outthink wounded game make him a valuable asset to any hunting party.

Curlies are found in the obedience and show rings, agility courses, hunt test arenas, tracking fields, and running flyball races. There are Curlies working as rescue dogs and as Helping Paws for disabled owners. We have Curlies working as therapy dogs visiting nursing homes and hospitals in many parts of the country. In Europe, they are accepted into the Seeing Eye program. However, the Curly's greatest desire is to belong to a loving family, taking part in every activity he can charm his way into.

The Curly, once referred to as a "meat hunter's dog," is agile and quite capable when it comes to recovering game, especially in water.

CURLIES IN THE FIELD

As you pull up to the boat ramp with your Curly sitting proudly in the boat ready for a day in the marsh, you will most likely receive many questioning glances from the other hunters around you. Just smile, and be ready to patiently answer their questions as to what kind of Poodle that is.

Because they are not common in the US, many

hunters have never heard of or seen a Curly-Coated Retriever. Once they hunt behind one, however, they will never forget him.

In waterfowl hunting, there is no comparison. The Curly will hunt in the coldest conditions and willingly break through the ice to retrieve a bird. He will swim and outwit the craftiest wounded duck and work the whole day just for the fun of it. Geese are no problem for the Curly because he knows no fear. A wounded goose stands no chance of escape.

In the field, the Curly is a close-quartering dog,

This trio of Curlies loves the outdoors and is ready for a hunting trip at a moment's notice.

excellent at tracking game, with the perseverance to stay on a fall until he finds it and returns it to you. The Curly may not be as flashy or fast as the Lab or Golden, but his intelligence and ability to learn and remember make him a dog that improves with every hunt.

After training several Curlies for us, a professional trainer said: "The Lab will do anything you ask of him, over and over again. The Curly will do anything you ask of him, but will ask you why!" That remark explains why those who hunt with Curlies are so sold on them. This independent dog can hunt and retrieve birds with little or no help from the handler, which makes him a

Whether in a group or on his own, the Curly's intelligence and ability to learn allows him to improve with every hunt.

great hunting companion for the hunter who wants to shoot his birds and depend on the dog to find and bring them back. The hunter who takes great pride in his ability to handle his dog to a kill will not appreciate this breed, as the Curly will usually ignore him and do the job as his nose tells him.

The Curly is easy to train and does not require many repetitive exercises once he learns what you want. Taking a young dog out for a hunt with an experienced dog will give the younger Curly more training in one afternoon than you alone could in weeks. Once he learns, he never forgets and only gets better at doing his job. Therefore, if you are looking for a smart and loyal hunting companion, the Curly may be just the dog for you.

CURLIES IN OBEDIENCE

Curly-Coated Retrievers are found training in obedience across the country. Although they are not the precise workers that some of the other breeds are, they do a credible job in the obedience ring and there are Obedience Trial Champions (OTCh.) both in AKC and UKC events. They train quite easily and love to work for you if you offer the right incentive. This differs with each dog. The biggest problem that Curly owners have is in keeping their dog's interest while training for precision, which can be successfully done with a little work. This is not a dog for the obedience trainer who does not wish to be challenged on every training day.

Opposite: This liver Curly holds the prey carefully in his mouth so as not to damage the flesh of the duck.

CURLIES IN AGILITY AND FLYBALL

Agility and flyball are newer sports that have recently come onto the scene and many people with many different breeds enjoy them. Agility encompasses speed, jumping ability, and the negotiation of obstacles all under the control of the handler. This is right up the Curly's alley. It is fun, challenging, and lets him display all of his physical and mental abilities. Those who take part in this new sport with their dogs really enjoy the fun and challenge. Again, training isn't always a breeze because the Curly does not fear anything and often wants to run the courses his way, which, of course, is unacceptable.

Flyball is a team event in which dogs run a series of jumps with a ball at the end of the course. The dog grabs the ball, returns back over the jumps, and then another team member does the same thing again. The event is timed and speed is of the essence. Curlies love it and we are seeing more Curlies as part of this team sport.

There are classes for both of these activities at many obedience-training facilities or in conjunction with local all-breed dog clubs across the country. They offer Curly owners a great way to work off some of their pet's energy needs while they both have fun.

Opposite: Along with being a talented hunter and retriever, the Curly-Coated Retriever is also one of the most obedient dogs and has won countless obedience trial championships and tracking certificates. Eclipse Ariel, here with her owner, Missy.

Am./Mex. Ch. Mayhem's Guilty As Charged, NA, WC, HC, CGC, FM, TT, TDI, aka "Charger," is also quite adept at flyball.

STANDARD FOR THE CURLY-COATED RETRIEVER

General Appearance—This smartly upstanding, multi-purpose hunting retriever is recognized by most canine historians as one of the oldest of the retrieving breeds. Developed in England, the Curly was long a favorite of English gamekeepers. Prized for innate field ability, courage and indomitable perseverance, a correctly built and tempered Curly will work as long as there is work to be done, retrieving both fur and feather in the heaviest of cover and the iciest of waters. To work all day, a Curly must be balanced and sound, strong and robust, and quick and agile. Outline, carriage and attitude all combine for a grace and elegance somewhat uncommon among the other retriever breeds, providing the unique, upstanding quality desired in the breed. In outline, the Curly is moderately angulated front and rear and, when comparing height to length, gives the impression of being higher on leg than the other retriever breeds. In carriage, the Curly is an erect, alert, self-confident dog. In motion, all parts blend into a smooth, powerful, harmonious symmetry. The coat, a hallmark of the breed, is of great importance for all Curlies, whether companion, hunting or show dogs. The perfect coat is a dense mass of small, tight, distinct, crisp curls. The Curly is wickedly smart and highly trainable and, as such, is cherished as much for his role as loyal companion at home as he is in the field.

Size, Proportion, Substance—Ideal height at withers: dogs, 25 to 27 inches; bitches, 23 to 25 inches. A

The size of the dog is important in the standard for the Curly, however, a superior dog should not be penalized if his size falls out of the average range.

clearly superior Curly that falls outside of this range should not be penalized because of size. The body proportions are slightly off square, meaning that the dog is slightly longer from prosternum to buttocks as he is from withers to ground. The Curly is both sturdy and elegant. The degree of substance is sufficient to ensure strength and endurance without sacrificing grace. Bone and substance are neither spindly nor massive and should be in proportion with weight and height and balanced throughout.

Head—The head is a longer-than-wide wedge, readily distinguishable from that of all other retriever breeds, and of a size in balance with the body. Length of foreface is equal, or nearly equal, to length of backskull and, when viewed in profile, the planes are parallel. The stop is shallow and sloping. At the point of joining, the width of foreface may be slightly less than the width of the backskull but blending of the two should be smooth. The head has a nearly straight, continuous taper to the nose and is clean cut, not coarse, blocky or cheeky. *Expression.* Intelligent and alert. *Eyes.* Almond-shaped, rather large but not too prominent. Black or brown in black dogs and brown or amber in liver dogs. Harsh yellow eyes and loose haws are undesirable. *Ears.* Rather small, set on a line slightly above the corner of the eye, and lying close to the head. *Backskull.* Flat or nearly flat. *Foreface.* Muzzle is wedge-shaped with no hint of snipiness. The taper ends mildly, neither acutely pointed nor bluntly squared-off but rather slightly rounding at the bottom. Mouth is level and never wry. Jaws are long and strong. A scissors bite is preferred. Teeth set straight and even. The lips are tight and

Opposite: Note the intelligent expression and the almond-shaped eyes typical of The Curly-Coated Retriever.

clean, not pendulous. The nose is fully pigmented; black on black dogs, brown on liver dogs. Nostrils are large.

Neck, Topline, Body—-*Neck.* Strong and slightly arched, of medium length, free from throatiness and flowing freely into moderately laid-back shoulders. *Backline.* The back, that portion of the body from the rear point of the withers to the beginning of the loin, is strong and level. The loin, that part of the body extending from the end of the rib cage to the start of the pelvis, is short and muscular. The croup, that portion of the body from the start of the pelvis to the tail set-on, is only slightly sloping. *Body.* Chest is decidedly deep and not too wide, oval in cross-section, with brisket reaching elbow. While the impression of the chest should be of depth not width, the chest is not pinched or narrow. The ribs are well-sprung, neither barrel-shaped nor slab-sided, and extend well back into a deep, powerful loin with a moderate tuck-up of flank. *Tail.* Carried straight or fairly straight, never docked, and reaching approximately to the hock. Never curled over the back and should not be kinked or crooked. Covered with curls and, if trimmed, tapering toward the point.

Forequarters—Shoulder blades are very long, well covered with muscle, and are moderately laid back at about a 55 degree angle. The width between shoulder blades is adequate to allow enough flexibility to easily retrieve game. Upper arm bones are about equal in length with shoulder blades and laid back at approximately the same angle as the blades, meaning the forelegs are set under the withers. The

This Curly has the correct deep chest, deep but not too wide. This helps him breathe well when working the field.

equal length of shoulder blade and upper arm bone and the balanced angulation between the two allows for good extension of the front legs. The forelegs are straight with strong, true pasterns. Feet are round and compact, with well-arched toes and thick pads. Front dewclaws are generally removed.

Hindquarters—Strong and in balance with front angulation. Thighs are powerful with muscling carrying well down into the second thigh. Stifle is of moderate bend. The hocks are strong and true, turning neither in nor out, with hock joint well let down. Rear dewclaws are generally removed.

Coat—The coat is a distinguishing characteristic and quite different from that of any other breed. The body coat is a thick mass of small, tight, crisp curls, lying close to the skin, resilient, water resistant, and of sufficient density to provide protection against weather, water and punishing cover. Curls also extend up the entire neck to the occiput, down the thigh and back leg to at least the hock, and over the entire tail. Elsewhere, the coat is short, smooth and straight, including on the forehead, face, front of forelegs, and feet. A patch of uncurled hair behind the withers or bald patches anywhere on the body, including bald strips down the back of the legs or a triangular bald patch on the throat, should be severely penalized. A looser, more open curl is acceptable on the ears. Sparse, silky, fuzzy or very harsh, dry or brittle hair is a fault. *Trimming.* Feathering may be trimmed from the ears, belly, backs of forelegs, thighs, pasterns, hocks, and feet. On the tail, feathering should be removed. Short

The curls of this dog's coat protect him against water, cold, and tough terrain while working for his hunting master.

These guys make for great family companions, as well as durable hunters and overall charming, intelligent dogs.

trimming of the coat on the ear is permitted but shearing of the body coat is undesirable.

Color—Black or liver. Either color is correct. A prominent white patch is undesirable but a few white hairs are allowable in an otherwise good dog.

Gait—The dual function of the Curly as both waterfowl retriever and upland game hunter demands a dog who moves with strength and power yet is quick and agile. The ground-covering stride is a well-coordinated melding of grace and power, neither mincing nor lumbering. The seemingly effortless trot is efficient and balanced front to rear. When viewed from the side, the reach in front and rear is free-flowing, not stilted or hackneyed. When viewed from the front or rear, movement is true: the front legs turn neither in nor out and the rear legs do not cross. Well-developed, muscular thighs and strong hocks do their full share of work, contributing to rear thrust and drive. The extension in front is strong and smooth and in balance with rear action. Balance in structure translates to balance in movement and is of great importance to ensure soundness and endurance; extremes of angulation and gait are not desirable.

Temperament—Self-confident, steadfast and proud, this active, intelligent dog is a charming and gentle family companion and a determined, durable hunter. The Curly is alert, biddable and responsive to family and friends, whether at home or in the field. Of independent nature and discerning intelligence, a Curly sometimes appears aloof or self-willed, and, as such, is often less demonstrative, particularly toward strangers, than the other retriever breeds. The Curly's independence and poise should not be confused with shyness or a lack of willingness to please. In the show ring, a correctly-tempered Curly will steadily stand his ground, submit easily to examination, and might or might not wag his tail when doing so. In the field, the Curly is eager, persistent and inherently courageous. At home, he is calm and affectionate. Shyness is a fault and any dog who shies away from show ring examination should be penalized. Minor allowances can be made for puppies who misbehave in the show ring due to overexuberance or lack of training or experience.

Approved 10/12/93
Effective 11/30/93

This pair of Curlies represents the only acceptable coat colors: liver and black.

GROOMING YOUR CURLY-COATED RETRIEVER

The Curly's coat is truly wash and wear. The hair on a correctly coated Curly will not grow longer than a couple of inches, and the curls will continue to wind around as a ram's horn does. A dog with looser curls will look shaggier if left ungroomed. Even so, his coat will only get so long. It will seem longer, however, because as the curl grows out it tends to loosen instead of getting tighter.

The Curly's coat should never be brushed or combed. This tends to stretch and frizz the coat. Because this is a single-coated breed, the Curly does not shed heavily year round, but he does regularly shed some as a natural growth process of hair. Spring is the time that all Curlies shed heavily and intact bitches shed after each season.

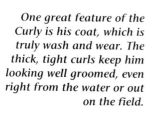

One great feature of the Curly is his coat, which is truly wash and wear. The thick, tight curls keep him looking well groomed, even right from the water or out on the field.

Regular bathing will help keep normal coat drop under control and your Curly companion smelling and feeling good. People with allergies should keep their Curly clean, as dust and pollens trapped in the coat are the very things to which their owners are sensitive. Curlies that are only bathed a few times a year tend to feel oily as the coat gets dirty, and dead hair and dirt accumulate in the coat.

A normal bathing routine would include the following: running through the coat with an undercoat rake before the bath; bathing with a pet shampoo and working the shampoo into the coat using a massaging action with your fingers to help loosen and bring the dead coat to the surface; a thorough rinsing and pat down with a towel; and a good shake or two by the dog and off to drip dry.

Curlies that are shown in conformation are trimmed to neaten up the dog's outline. The excess hair on the back of the front and rear legs, between the toes, over the shoulders, and the underside of the neck, chest, and stomach should be trimmed town. Unruly curls sticking out on the body may be nipped back to be even with the rest of the body coat. The flagging on the tail is trimmed off, leaving the tail an even length all over with a slight taper to the end. The ears can get quite shaggy as the curl is usually looser and should be shortened all over, and the edges of the ear trimmed even with the ear leathers. The overall length of the body coat should not be trimmed down. A more open-coated Curly will generally look neater and a bit curlier if the body coat is trimmed shorter a few times a year.

Most hunters do not bathe their Curlies during hunting season so that the dead hair accumulation remains in the coat for more protection in the field. It is said that a well-coated Curly can be hunted and shown at the same time, and the lack of dead coat does not hinder the dogs in the field. If you want to clean your companion during hunting season, do so.

Nails should be trimmed on a regular basis because the quick, or vein in the nail, grows as fast as the nail on most Curlies. If left untrimmed for even a few weeks, the nails will have grown too long and will be difficult to trim back to where they belong. A dog with nice, tight feet will need less attention to nail trimming. It is important to trim your puppy's nails regularly from the very beginning, as most Curlies don't particularly like having it done and should get used to the process

Opposite: Hunting involves plenty of action and exercise, as well as occasionally working in wet, muddy conditions. Most hunters let their Curlies go without a bath through the hunting season so that the dead hair accumulates in the coat and helps protect the dog.

The Curly's distinctive coat is a distinguishing characteristic that provides protection against weather and water and requires little grooming.

from a very young age.

Ears should be wiped out with an ear cleaner or alcohol on a cotton ball regularly to keep excess wax under control. If your dog is swimming a lot, and especially during hunting season, the ears should be cleaned on a daily basis.

Just as a reminder to hunters: All dogs should be checked for debris in the coat and ears after each hunt, and you should also check for cuts or abrasions on the body, ears, and feet so that they can be treated immediately. Curlies do not tend to fuss over minor injuries, so be vigilant and catch them before they can get infected or affect your dog's ability to hunt on another day.

BREED CONCERNS

Curly-Coated Retrievers seem to be a hardy breed. Unlike some of the other retrievers, Curlies as a whole seem to suffer a lower incidence of genetically related problems. Even so, when talking with a breeder, ask about potential health problems in the breed and specifically in their lines. If the breeder says there are none, *beware!*

A reputable breeder will be happy to discuss potential problems in the breed, especially those that may be a problem in their own lines. They should also tell you what health screening they do with their breeding stock and explain their guarantees.

If your Curly should develop a major health problem, contact your breeder and give him/her all the information you can. This way your breeder can be

A perfect 10! A healthy Curly can participate in any activity—even diving!

better informed about potential problems in their line and adjust their breeding programs.

CANCER

Lately, an increasing number of Curlies have been diagnosed with various forms of cancer. The genetics of cancer is relatively unknown and it is believed that environment has a lot to do with how widespread the problem seems to be in all pets. Curlies don't seem to be predisposed to any particular type of cancer, so there hasn't been any genetic link identified with the breed.

SEIZURES

Another problem becoming more common in all breeds is seizure. Environmental factors, as well as health problems, can lead to a dog having seizures. Most of the time, diagnosis and treatment of the underlying problem will end the seizures.

Idiopathic epilepsy is seizuring in which no identifiable physical cause can be found. This type of seizure is believed to be inherited, and although it can usually be controlled with medication, sometimes nothing seems to help.

Your Curly-Coated Retriever's gait should be free and powerful. All Curlies should be screened free of hip dysplasia before being bred.

There has been a very low incidence of seizures in Curlies and at this time, there is no type of screening available to identify the problem in our breeding stock.

HIP DYSPLASIA (HD)

Hip dysplasia is a malformation of the ball and socket joint of the hip with varying degrees of impairment. A dog with a minor degree of dysplasia may lead a normal life with little or no pain or discomfort. Depending on the degree of impairment, a dysplastic dog may begin to show signs of a problem even as a puppy, but most of the time the damage doesn't become evident or hamper the dog's lifestyle until later in life. HD is inherited and affected dogs should not be bred.

The only way to properly diagnose HD is by X-ray, or a new process called Penn-Hip™. The X-ray taken by the veterinarian is sent to OFA (Orthopedic Foundation of America) for grading. Three board-certified veterinarians read the X-ray and a grade of Excellent, Good, or Fair is given to those hips that pass. Otherwise, a non-passing certification is given with a grading on the degree of impairment.

ELBOW DYSPLASIA (ED)

Elbow dysplasia includes several problems that include ununited anconeal process, fragmented coronoid process, and osteochondrosis dessicans. Many times, dogs with these problems show gait abnormalities or lameness as puppies. Again, X-rays are used for proper diagnosis of ED.

Your Curly must be 24 months old to have the OFA pass on hip and elbow X-rays. If a problem is suspected, X-rays should be done earlier. The breeding of stock under the age of two is risky, as the development of the hips is not complete and OFA will not certify before the age of two. If the breeder says the dogs have been X-rayed but have no OFA certificate, *beware*.

Although HD and ED are not a big problem in Curlies, it is important for the parents of your puppy to have an OFA certification, a copy of which should be included in your puppy packet.

Note: Because X-raying for ED has only been done for the past few years, older breeding stock may not have been X-rayed for ED while their hips were certified. According to OFA, there has been no incidence of ED in Curlies who have been X-rayed to date, so there is little reason for concern if your puppy's parents do not have the ED certification.

EYE PROBLEMS

Cataracts of various kinds, corneal dystrophy, and progressive retinal atrophy (PRA) are problems that can lead to possible blindness later in your pet's life. These problems can be screened for by an AVCO-certified veterinary opthomalogist. Screening should be done yearly on breeding stock and a CERF (Canine Eye Registration Foundation) certification should be provided to all new puppy owners.

Distichiasis (extra eyelashes), entropion (eyelids rolling inward), and ectropion (eyelids that droop outward), are genetically inherited so you should be aware of the problem if it exists in the line you choose, though it will not usually impair the normal life of an affected dog.

While none of these problems are life threatening, there has been some incidence of all of these problems in Curlies. Be sure to ask for a copy of the CERF for both the sire and dam and be sure that it is up to date, as some of these problems do not show up in screening until the dogs are older.

PATTERNED BALDNESS

The most widespread problem in Curlies is patterned baldness. It usually manifests itself as bilateral bald patches or stripes on the back of the rear legs, the throat, the sides of the neck, behind the shoulders, or in less severely affected dogs, as thin, brittle, uncurled hair all over the body.

Puppies may sometimes have good coats when young and the patterning does not show up until sexual maturity. Even when the parents have good coats, they can produce patterned puppies, so it is important that the breeder knows his or her lines for several generations back. The genetics of the problem are unclear and often misdiagnosed by vets. Supplements, special diets, and even neutering doesn't seem to help. Often, secondary problems attributed to auto immune deficiencies and reproductive problems manifest themselves in severely affected dogs.

Curlies that are only mildly affected will live normal, healthy lives with only some patterning or incorrect coat type. This coat problem is not life threatening, but affected dogs should not be bred.

SELECTING A CURLY-COATED RETRIEVER

Because Curlies are quite rare in this country, it will not be as easy to locate puppies or adults as other breeds. The Curly-Coated Retriever Club of America (CCRCA) will send an information packet along with a list of breeders on request. Members of the CCRCA may be placed on this list for a fee, so the list changes each year, as those planning a breeding during that year make sure to be on the list.

Hunting magazines and the dog-related magazines found on your newsstand often advertise litters. If there is a dog show nearby, you might find a Curly owner there who will talk to you and give you information about available litters.

Hunting dog magazines will often carry the names of respected breeders that produce Curly-Coated Retrievers that possess both work instincts and good temperament.

CURLY RESCUE

The CCRCA has an active rescue program, and this may be a good way to acquire your Curly. Dogs, usually older pups or adults, are fostered into volunteer homes. Their health, physical condition, temperament, and habits are evaluated and a recommendation as to the type of home that will be most suitable for them is made. The goal of rescue is to place these dogs in homes where they will fit into the owner's lifestyle and thus have a family to love for a lifetime.

If you contact the CCRCA rescue to inquire about acquiring a Curly, be ready to answer some questions about yourself, your family, your experience in dogs, your lifestyle, etc. These questions help in the placement of the dog. If there is a Curly for you to consider, a complete history will be provided and you may choose to take that dog or wait for another.

A great way of ensuring that you will get a quality Curly is to study the history of the pup, as well as examining the parents and other dogs of the same line.

To get information on Curly breeders or rescue, write to the following address: Sheila Callahan-Young, CCRCA Recording Secretary, 3 Roberts Ct., Gloucester, MA, 01930.

TALKING TO A BREEDER

When contacting a breeder about a potential puppy or adult, you should have an idea of what your preferences are in a pet. Things like color, sex, temperament, reasons for getting a Curly (hunting, obedience, pet, show, etc.), ability and time to train and exercise a Curly, and housing will be questions asked of you by the breeder. These are all-important factors in determining whether they have a puppy for you.

Ask Questions

When inquiring about a prospective puppy or adult, please keep the following points in mind:

1. Be sure that both parents are OFA certified. It is preferable to know the status of the grandparents as well.

2. Be sure that both parents have valid CERF numbers. These should be less than a year old. This certifies their eyes as being clear of defects at a particular time. If the dogs are under five years of age, ask about the grandparents' CERF numbers, too.

3. Coat patterning is a problem in this breed. If the parents are even a little patterned or do not have a good coat, be aware that the puppies may also have coat problems when they grow up. The coat should be curled all over the body and have density. You will find that puppies sometimes have curls on the top of their

When meeting with a breeder, it's always a good idea to ask questions about his or her overall breeding program, as well as about the parents and the litter itself.

heads that go away as they get older.

4. Observe the parents as well as the puppies for temperament. A shy or skittish parent can produce a problem puppy. The dogs don't have to be overly outgoing, but they should not be afraid to be around you. The puppies are usually more interested in themselves, though they should take time to check you out and not run or hide from you.

5. Retrieving instinct should be noticeable in six-week-old puppies. Watch how they play and see if you can get them to play a retrieving game with you. They should not have a problem with picking up and carrying objects, or even bringing them back to you on occasion.

6. Talk to the breeder and ask why he/she bred this litter. Were they trying to improve what they have in both conformation and hunting ability? Do you get the impression they are just out to sell puppies? Be wary of people who do not put research into their breedings. What did they get in the litter that they like? What don't they like? Have them analyze their puppies, especially the one in which you are interested.

8. It may be that you will do your interviewing over the phone. Ask for pictures or videos of the puppies and parents. Get answers to your questions and be honest in answering the questions the breeder asks. Get copies of OFAs, CERFs, and the pedigree with those pictures. Don't decide sight unseen—this goes with the purchase of an adult as well.

9. Don't shy away from a spay/neuter agreement when buying a pet puppy. This isn't always something that is required, but many breeders place their pet puppies this way. It protects against possible breedings of Curlies that should not be bred. This is important if you are to keep the qualities that attracted you to this breed.

10. Remember, don't rush the decision to purchase a puppy. Take time to think about it; 24 hours is a reasonable amount of time to request that the breeder hold a puppy for you. If you make such a request, be considerate enough to let the breeder know of your decision either way.

11. Ask about health problems afflicting the parents and grandparents. This may include seizures, auto immune problems, skin or coat problems not associated with patterning, thyroid imbalances, heart problems, tumors in aging dogs, allergies, bloat or torsion, etc. These are not necessarily common problems in

363

Curlies but are found to some degree in almost all breeds. It is helpful to know the background of the parents so that you are prepared if a problem crops up with your puppy. Problems sometimes just happen and there may be no prior reason for them.

12. Get information on grooming your Curly. Although these dogs are essentially wash-and-wear dogs, there are some grooming techniques that help keep your Curly looking like the ones in the show ring.

13. If you plan to show your puppy, will the breeder

If you've seen a litter that you like, it is reasonable to ask the breeder to hold a particular puppy for 24 hours so that you have time to consider the purchase.

Socialization with people and other dogs is an important aspect in raising your new Curly puppy.

help you learn to present your Curly? Will the breeder show him for you? What does the breeder expect of you if the puppy is to be shown? Are you willing to keep a prospective show puppy sexually complete until the dog finishes his championship or is campaigned?

14. If you want a puppy to breed, find out what the breeder expects from you, and what control, if any, does he have in the breeding of your puppy. Remember that the Curly-Coated Retriever is not numerous in the US, the gene pool is small, and your reasons for breeding the Curly—and which dog you breed to— are very important to the future of this breed. Because of these factors, many breeders will insist on some control of your breeding program at least until they are sure of your knowledge and ability.

15. How does your breeder recommend socializing your puppy? Are you willing to put the time into this process? Socialization of even a pet puppy is very important. You wouldn't have gotten interested in a Curly if the first one you saw had bad manners and was uncomfortable outside of his own home. Curlies are very family-oriented dogs, but they should be able to get along comfortably in an unfamiliar environment with people and other animals. Socialization is a never-ending task.

DISTANT LITTERS

Once you have located an available litter, you may find that the breeder is not local. This could mean quite a drive for your family to see the litter, or it may mean that you will have to trust the breeder to send you a puppy sight unseen. This often happens with

Curlies because the breeders are sparsely located all over the country. If you really want to see the puppies, patience is the key, as a local breeder may not be planning a litter when you contact them.

AIR TRAVEL

If you decide to purchase a puppy from a distant breeder, your only method of shipment may be by air. This can be done safely, quickly, and with little trauma to the puppy.

The best way is to have the puppy flown as excess baggage with someone you know. Unfortunately, this is not an option most of the time. So, if the puppy will be shipped alone, check the airlines and find a direct flight from point of origin to point of delivery. Fly the puppy *over the counter*, which is a bit more expensive, though the waiting time in baggage is much less and your puppy will be delivered to you at the airline's baggage pick-up area instead of at the freight office.

It may be a longer drive to pick up your puppy at a major airport, but there is less risk of the puppy missing a connecting flight or suffering through a long delay at a connecting airport. The new owner must pay the price of the crate and shipping, over and above the price of the puppy.

Another issue in shipping is the time of year. Cold and heat (temperatures at origin and destination) may mean more inconvenient arrival times or postponing shipment because it is either too cold or too hot. This is something that needs to be taken into consideration when planning your shipment. I have flown both adult dogs and puppies across the country and they all did very well, with no bad side effects. The key is in the planning.

Because this is such a rare breed, there are not always puppies available when you would like them. Think twice before getting a puppy from someone who always has a litter ready for purchase. Listen carefully to the breeder's answer to the question of why he bred this litter. Reputable breeders always try to improve the quality of their stock, not make as many puppies as possible. Ask for references of others who have purchased their puppies and check them. Also, ask for a veterinary reference to check on the care of their animals. Above all, be willing to wait for a puppy. You won't be sorry if you find a breeder with whom you are comfortable and are willing to wait for their next litter.

SHOWING YOUR CURLY-COATED RETRIEVER

Ch. Ptarmigan Gale at Riverwatch, CD, collects her 1997 CCRCA National Specialty award. She was bred by Janean Marti (Ptarmigan) and is owned by authors Gary and Mary Meek (Riverwatch).

Do you think you'd like to own and show a Curly? Great! Here are a few things you should know about showing dogs.

First, go to shows and look at Curlies; there are different types (looks) and only you can decide which look you like best. Then buy the best puppy you can afford from a proven show breeder that produces the look you want.

Since type is not the only important thing, study the standard for the breed and ask questions. It takes more than just a pretty dog to win at shows. Learn how size, substance, bone, coat, soundness, temperament, and type all go together to make a functional, handsome Curly.

Tell the breeders you talk to what you would like to do with your show dog and find a breeder with whom you are comfortable enough to spend time listening and learning.

SOCIALIZATION

After you purchase your show-prospect Curly, begin socializing him immediately. Find a handling class for beginners after he has received all of his shots and learn how to present your puppy as you teach him the ropes. Then, go to some fun matches so both of you can experience the show atmosphere and become more comfortable in the ring.

After your puppy has reached the age of six months, you can enter him into regular AKC shows. Your breeder can be of help to you in choosing which shows to enter and as a source of information on where other Curlies will be competing. Have fun— puppyhood is when you and your Curly should have a good time at shows, so you can laugh and learn from mistakes in the ring.

CONDITIONING

One of the most important things that those who are new to showing must understand is the need to condition your dog. A show dog needs to be in the same optimum physical and mental condition that a working Curly must be in to hunt day after day. This requires good food, attention to health issues, and daily physical exercise. The type of exercise will be different with the age of your dog. Muscles must be built and maintained, just as a human athlete does to be competitive. This takes time and effort, and if you don't have the time, your Curly won't be competitive when shown. It takes more than just a good pedigree and a pretty face to make a successful show dog.

As with any hobby, showing dogs can be an exciting and enjoyable way to spend your free time. It is also an expensive hobby, and because Curlies are not found at every show, it takes some traveling to get to where there will be points available. If, because of time constraints, you are unwilling to drive a distance

When showing your Curly, the experience should be fun for both you and your dog. Be prepared to learn from your mistakes and to help your dog learn what is expected of him.

to shows, it may take quite a while to finish your dog. Alternatively, you will have to send him with someone else, meaning your dog will have to spend time away from you and your family while he is being shown. These are all things to take into consideration before choosing to show a dog.

You should be aware that showing your dog is not only an exciting hobby, but is also an expensive one. Traveling, hard work, and more are all part of the game, but the benefits are worth it!

YOUR PUPPY'S NEW HOME

Before actually collecting your puppy, it is better that you purchase the basic items you will need in advance of the pup's arrival date. This allows you more opportunity to shop around and ensure that you have exactly what you want rather than having to buy lesser quality in a hurry.

It is always better to collect the puppy as early in the day as possible. In most instances this will mean that the puppy has a few hours with your family before it is time to retire for his first night's sleep away from his former home.

Your new puppy will be anxious and unsure about his new surroundings on the first night in your home. Be patient and caring and he will soon adjust.

If the breeder is local, then you may not need any form of box to place the puppy in when you bring him home. A member of the family can hold the pup in his lap—duly protected by some towels just in case the puppy becomes car sick! Be sure to advise the breeder at what time you hope to arrive for the puppy, as this will obviously influence the feeding of the pup that morning or afternoon. If you arrive early in the day, then they will likely only give the pup a light breakfast so as to reduce the risk of travel sickness.

If the trip will be of a few hours duration, you should take a travel crate with you. The crate will provide your pup with a safe place to lie down and rest during the trip. During the trip, the puppy will no doubt wish to relieve his bowels, so you will have to make a few stops. On a long journey you may need a rest yourself, and can take the opportunity to let the puppy get some fresh air. However, do not let the puppy walk where there may have been a lot of other dogs because he might pick up an infection. Also, if he relieves his bowels at such a time, do not just leave the feces where they were dropped. This is the height of irresponsibility. It has resulted in many public parks and other places actually banning dogs. You can purchase poop-scoops from your pet shop and should have them with you whenever you are taking the dog out where he might foul a public place.

Your journey home should be made as quickly as possible. If it is a hot day, be sure the car interior is amply supplied with fresh air. It should never be too hot or too cold for the puppy. The pup must never be placed where he might be subject to a draft. If the journey requires an overnight stop at a motel, be aware that other guests will not appreciate a puppy

Puppies love to investigate and explore their new home and the surrounding territory. Let them be, though you should monitor and protect them from potential danger.

crying half the night. You must regard the puppy as a baby and comfort him so he does not cry for long periods. The worst thing you can do is to shout at or smack him. This will mean your relationship is off to a really bad start. You wouldn't smack a baby, and your puppy is still very much just this.

ON ARRIVING HOME

By the time you arrive home the puppy may be very tired, in which case he should be taken to his sleeping area and allowed to rest. Children should not be allowed to interfere with the pup when he is sleeping. If the pup is not tired, he can be allowed to investigate his new home—but always under your close supervision. After a short look around, the puppy will no doubt appreciate a light meal and a drink of water. Do not overfeed him at his first meal because he will be in an excited state and more likely to be sick.

Although it is an obvious temptation, you should not invite friends and neighbors around to see the

Try not to invite friends and neighbors over to see your new addition for at least a few days. This will help your puppy acclimate himself to his new home and generally settle down.

new arrival until he has had at least 48 hours in which to settle down. Indeed, if you can delay this longer then do so, especially if the puppy is not fully vaccinated. At the very least, the visitors might introduce some local bacteria on their clothing that the puppy is not immune to. This aspect is always a risk when a pup has been moved some distance, so the fewer people the pup meets in the first week or so the better.

DANGERS IN THE HOME

Your home holds many potential dangers for a little mischievous puppy, so you must think about these in advance and be sure he is protected from them. The more obvious are as follows:

Open Fires. All open fires should be protected by a mesh screen guard so there is no danger of the pup being burned by spitting pieces of coal or wood.

Electrical Wires. Puppies just love chewing on things, so be sure that all electrical appliances are neatly hidden from view and are not left plugged in when not in use. It is not sufficient simply to turn the plug switch to the off position—pull the plug from the socket.

Open Doors. A door would seem a pretty innocuous object, yet with a strong draft it could kill or injure a puppy easily if it is slammed shut. Always ensure there is no risk of this happening. It is most likely during warm weather when you have windows or outside doors open and a sudden gust of wind blows through.

Balconies. If you live in a high-rise building, obviously the pup must be protected from falling. Be sure he cannot get through any railings on your patio, balcony, or deck.

Ponds and Pools. A garden pond or a swimming pool is a very dangerous place for a little puppy to be near. Be sure it is well screened so there is no risk of the pup falling in. It takes barely a minute for a pup—or a child—to drown.

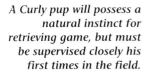

A Curly pup will possess a natural instinct for retrieving game, but must be supervised closely his first times in the field.

The Kitchen. While many puppies will be kept in the kitchen, at least while they are toddlers and not able to control their bowel movements, this is a room full of

danger—especially while you are cooking. When cooking, keep the puppy in a play pen or in another room where he is safely out of harm's way. Alternatively, if you have a carry box or crate, put him in this so he can still see you but is well protected.

Dog ownership can teach children how to properly respect and care for animals. Charger and Missy are the best of friends.

Be aware, when using washing machines, that more than one puppy has clambered in and decided to have a nap and received a wash instead! If you leave the washing machine door open and leave the room for any reason, then be sure to check inside the machine before you close the door and switch on.

Small Children. Toddlers and small children should never be left unsupervised with puppies. In spite of such advice it is amazing just how many people not only do this but also allow children to pull and maul pups. They should be taught from the outset that a puppy is not a plaything to be dragged about the home—and they should be promptly scolded if they disobey.

Children must be shown how to lift a puppy so it is safe. Failure by you to correctly educate your children about dogs could one day result in their getting a very nasty bite or scratch. When a puppy is lifted, his weight must always be supported. To lift the pup, first place your right hand under his chest. Next, secure the pup by using your left hand to hold his neck. Now you can lift him and bring him close to your chest. Never lift a pup by his ears and, while he can be lifted by the scruff of his neck where the fur is loose, there is no reason ever to do this, so don't.

Beyond the dangers already cited you may be able to think of other ones that are specific to your home—steep basement steps or the like. Go around your home and check out all potential problems—you'll be glad you did.

THE FIRST NIGHT

The first few nights a puppy spends away from his mother and littermates are quite traumatic for him. He will feel very lonely, maybe cold, and will certainly miss the heartbeat of his siblings when sleeping. To help overcome his loneliness it may help to place a clock next to his bed—one with a loud tick. This will in some way soothe him, as the clock ticks to a rhythm not dissimilar from a heart beat. A cuddly toy may also help in the first few weeks. A dim nightlight may provide some comfort to the puppy, because his eyes will not yet be fully able to see in the dark. The puppy may want to leave his bed for a drink or to relieve himself.

If the pup does whimper in the night, there are two things you should not do. One is to get up and chastise him, because he will not understand why you are shouting at him; and the other is to rush to comfort him every time he cries because he will quickly realize that if he wants you to come running all he needs to do is to holler loud enough!

By all means give your puppy some extra attention on his first night, but after this quickly refrain from doing so . The pup will cry for a while but then settle down and go to sleep. Some pups are, of course, worse than others in this respect, so you must use balanced judgment in the matter. Many owners take their pups to bed with them, and there is certainly nothing wrong with this.

The pup will be no trouble in such cases. However, you should only do this if you intend to let this be a permanent arrangement, otherwise it is hardly fair to the puppy. If you have decided to have two puppies, then they will keep each other company and you will have few problems.

OTHER PETS

If you have other pets in the home then the puppy must be introduced to them under careful supervision. Puppies will get on just fine with any other pets—but you must make due allowance for the respective

Puppies are used to sleeping with their mother and other littermates, so sleeping alone in your home may frighten him. Pay extra attention to him for the first few days.

sizes of the pets concerned, and appreciate that your puppy has a rather playful nature. It would be very foolish to leave him with a young rabbit. The pup will want to play and might bite the bunny and get altogether too rough with it. Kittens are more able to defend themselves from overly cheeky pups, who will get a quick scratch if they overstep the mark. The adult cat could obviously give the pup a very bad scratch, though generally cats will jump clear of pups and watch them from a suitable vantage point. Eventually they will meet at ground level where the cat will quickly hiss and box a puppy's ears. The pup will soon learn to respect an adult cat; thereafter they will probably develop into great friends as the pup matures into an adult dog.

HOUSETRAINING

Undoubtedly, the first form of training your puppy will undergo is in respect to his toilet habits. To achieve this you can use either newspaper, or a large litter tray filled with soil or lined with newspaper. A puppy cannot control his bowels until he is a few months old, and not fully until he is an adult. Therefore you must anticipate his needs and be prepared for a few accidents. The prime times a pup will urinate and defecate are shortly after he wakes up from a sleep, shortly after he has eaten, and after he has been playing awhile. He will usually whimper and start searching the room for a suitable place. You must quickly pick him up and place him on the newspaper or in the litter tray. Hold him in position gently but firmly. He might jump out of the box without doing anything on the first one or two occasions, but if you simply repeat the procedure every time you think he wants to relieve himself then eventually he will get the message.

When he does defecate as required, give him

plenty of praise, telling him what a good puppy he is. The litter tray or newspaper must, of course, be cleaned or replaced after each use—puppies do not like using a dirty toilet any more than you do. The pup's toilet can be placed near the kitchen door and as he gets older the tray can be placed outside while the door is open. The pup will then start to use it while he is outside. From that time on, it is easy to get the pup to use a given area of the yard.

Many breeders recommend the popular alternative of crate training. Upon bringing the pup home, introduce him to his crate. The open wire crate is the best choice, placed in a restricted, draft-free area of the home. Put the pup's Nylabone® and other favorite toys in the crate along with a wool blanket or other suitable bedding. The puppy's natural cleanliness instincts prohibit him from soiling in the place where he sleeps, his crate. The puppy should be allowed to go in and out of the open crate during the day, but he should sleep in the crate at the night and at other intervals during the day. Whenever the pup is taken out of his crate, he should be brought outside (or to his newspapers) to do his business. Never use the crate as a place of punishment. You will see how quickly your pup takes to his crate, considering it as his own safe haven from the big world around him.

THE EARLY DAYS

You will no doubt be given much advice on how to bring up your puppy. This will come from dog-owning friends, neighbors, and through articles and books you may read on the subject. Some of the advice will be sound, some will be nothing short of rubbish. What you should do above all else is to keep an open mind and let common sense prevail over prejudice and worn-out ideas that have been handed down over the

When it comes to housetraining, keep your puppy confined to a specific area so that accidents will not happen where you don't want them to. Crate training is an excellent method of housebreaking.

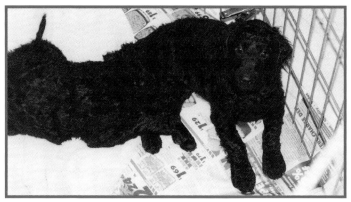

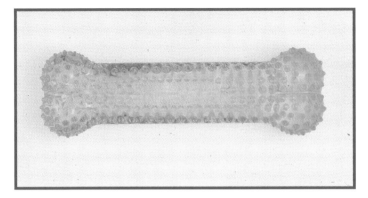

The Plaque Attacker™ is safe for aggressive chewers and provides hours of enjoyment. The raised dental tips help to combat plaque and tartar on the surface of your Curly's teeth.

centuries. There is no one way that is superior to all others, no more than there is no one dog that is exactly a replica of another. Each is an individual and must always be regarded as such.

A dog never becomes disobedient, unruly, or a menace to society without the full consent of his owner. Your puppy may have many limitations, but the singular biggest limitation he is confronted with in so many instances is his owner's inability to understand his needs and how to cope with them.

IDENTIFICATION

It is a sad reflection on our society that the number of dogs and cats stolen every year runs into many thousands. To these can be added the number that get lost. If you do not want your cherished pet to be lost or stolen, then you should see that he is carrying a permanent identification number, as well as a temporary tag on his collar.

Permanent markings come in the form of tattoos placed either inside the pup's ear flap, or on the inner side of a pup's upper rear leg. The number given is then recorded with one of the national registration companies. Research laboratories will not purchase dogs carrying numbers as they realize these are clearly someone's pet, and not abandoned animals. As a result, thieves will normally abandon dogs so marked and this at least gives the dog a chance to be taken to the police or the dog pound, when the number can be traced and the dog reunited with its family. The only problem with this method at this time is that there are a number of registration bodies, so it is not always apparent which one the dog is registered with (as you provide the actual number). However, each registration body is aware of his competitors and will normally be happy to supply their addresses. Those holding

If you allow your dog to run free, make sure to have the proper tags on his collar in case he escapes your view and gets lost. Because so many dogs are lost or stolen each year, you should do everything in your power to protect him.

the dog can check out which one you are with. It is not a perfect system, but until such is developed it's the best available.

Another permanent form of identification is the microchip, a computer that is no bigger than a grain of rice that is injected between the dog's shoulder blades. The dog feels no discomfort. The dog also receives a tag that says he is microchipped. If the dog is lost and picked up by the humane society, they can trace the owner by scanning the microchip. It is the safest form of identification.

A temporary tag takes the form of a metal or plastic disk large enough for you to place the dog's name and your phone number on it—maybe even your address as well. In virtually all places you will be required to obtain a license for your puppy. This may not become applicable until the pup is six months old, but it might apply regardless of his age. Much depends upon the state within a country, or the country itself, so check with your veterinarian if the breeder has not already advised you on this.

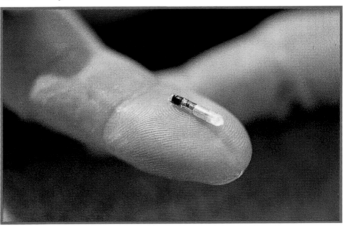

The newest method of identification is microchipping. The microchip is no bigger than a grain of rice and is painlessly inserted underneath the skin of your Curly.

FEEDING YOUR CURLY-COATED RETRIEVER

Dog owners today are fortunate in that they live in an age where considerable cash has been invested in the study of canine nutritional requirements. This means dog food manufacturers are very concerned about ensuring that their foods are of the best quality. The result of all of their studies, apart from the food itself, is that dog owners are bombarded with advertisements telling them why they must purchase a given brand. The number of products available to you is unlimited, so it is hardly surprising to find that dogs in general suffer from obesity and an excess of vitamins, rather than the reverse. Be sure to feed your dog age-appropriate food—puppy food up to one year of age, adult food thereafter. Generally, breeders recommend dry food supplemented by canned, if needed.

FACTORS AFFECTING NUTRITIONAL NEEDS

Activity Level. A dog that lives in a country environment and is able to exercise for long periods of the day will need more food than the same breed of dog living in an apartment and given little exercise.

Quality of the Food. Obviously the quality of food will affect the quantity required by a puppy. If the nutritional content of a food is low then the puppy will need more of it than if a better quality food was fed.

Balance of Nutrients and Vitamins. Feeding a puppy the correct balance of nutrients is not easy because the average person is not able to measure out ratios of one to another, so it is a case of trying

Curly-Coated Retrievers are energetic and active dogs and need a diet appropriate for their needs. In other words, Flint, the Curly, burns plenty of calories when pulling his friend, Emily, the Pug, and requires proper nutrition.

to see that nothing is in excess. However, only tests, or your veterinarian, can be the source of reliable advice.

Genetic and Biological Variation. Apart from all of the other considerations, it should be remembered that each puppy is an individual. His genetic make-up will influence not only his physical characteristics but also his metabolic efficiency. This being so, two pups from the same litter can vary quite a bit in the amount of food they need to perform the same function under the same conditions. If you consider the potential combinations of all of these factors then you will see that pups of a given breed could vary quite a bit in the amount of food they will need. Before discussing feeding quantities it is valuable to know at least a little about the composition of food and its role in the body.

COMPOSITION AND ROLE OF FOOD
The main ingredients of food are protein, fats, and

carbohydrates, each of which is needed in relatively large quantities when compared to the other needs of vitamins and minerals. The other vital ingredient of food is, of course, water. Although all foods obviously contain some of the basic ingredients needed for an animal to survive, they do not all contain the ingredients in the needed ratios or type. For example, there are many forms of protein, just as there are many types of carbohydrates. Both of these compounds are found in meat and in vegetable matter—but not all of those that are needed will be in one particular meat or vegetable. Plants, especially, do not contain certain amino acids that are required for the synthesis of certain proteins needed by dogs.

Likewise, vitamins are found in meats and vegetable matter, but vegetables are a richer source of most. Meat contains very little carbohydrates. Some vitamins can be synthesized by the dog, so they do not need to be supplied via the food. Dogs are carnivores and this means their digestive tract has evolved to need a high quantity of meat as compared to humans. The digestive system of carnivores is unable to break down the tough cellulose walls of plant matter, but it is easily able

The main necessities in your Curly's diet are protein, fats, and carbohydrates. Of course, water is an essential ingredient to good health for any living thing.

This is a healthful flavored treat for your Curly-Coated Retriever. Its bone-hard structure helps control plaque mechanically. It becomes a rich cracker that he will love after it is microwaved.

to assimilate proteins from meat.

In order to gain its needed vegetable matter in a form that it can cope with, the carnivore eats all of its prey. This includes the partly digested food within the stomach. In commercially prepared foods, the cellulose is broken down by cooking. During this process the vitamin content is either greatly reduced or lost altogether. The manufacturer therefore adds vitamins once the heat process has been completed. This is why commercial foods are so useful as part of a feeding regimen, providing they are of good quality and from a company that has prepared the foods very carefully.

Proteins

These are made from amino acids, of which at least ten are essential if a puppy is to maintain healthy growth. Proteins provide the building blocks for the puppy's body. The richest sources are meat, fish, and poultry, together with their by-products. The latter will include milk, cheese, yogurt, fishmeal, and eggs. Vegetable matter that has a high protein content includes soy beans, together with numerous corn and other plant extracts that have been dehydrated. The actual protein content needed in the diet will be determined both by the activity level of the dog and his age. The total protein need will also be influenced by the digestibility factor of the food given.

Fats

These serve numerous roles in the puppy's body.

They provide insulation against the cold, and help buffer the organs from knocks and general activity shocks. They provide the richest source of energy, and reserves of this, and they are vital in the transport of vitamins and other nutrients, via the blood, to all other organs. Finally, it is the fat content within a diet that gives it palatability. It is important that the fat content of a diet should not be excessive. This is because the high energy content of fats (more than twice that of protein or carbohydrate) will increase the overall energy content of the diet. The puppy will adjust his food intake to that of his energy needs, which are obviously more easily met in a high-energy diet. This will mean that while the fats are providing the energy needs of the puppy, the over-all diet may not be providing his protein, vitamin, and mineral needs, so signs of protein deficiency will become apparent. Rich sources of fats are meat, their byproducts (butter, milk), and vegetable oils, such as safflower, olive, corn, or soy bean.

Carbohydrates

These are the principal energy compounds given to puppies and adult dogs. Their inclusion within most commercial brand dog foods is for cost, rather than dietary needs. These compounds are more commonly known as sugars, and they are seen in simple or complex compounds of carbon, hydrogen, and oxygen. One of the simple sugars is called glucose, and it is vital

The age and activity level of your Curly will determine his nutritional needs. Your breeder should provide you with a diet sheet for your new puppy. If not, or if you want to change his diet, consult your veterinarian first.

Good nutrition will be evident in your Curly's shiny coat and high energy level.

to many metabolic processes. When large chains of glucose are created, they form compound sugars. One of these is called glycogen, and it is found in the cells of animals. Another, called starch, is the material that is found in the cells of plants.

Vitamins

These are not foods as such but chemical compounds that assist in all aspects of an animal's life. They help in so many ways that to attempt to describe these effectively would require a chapter in itself. Fruits are a rich source of vitamins, as is the liver of most animals. Many vitamins are unstable and easily destroyed by light, heat, moisture, or rancidity. An excess of vitamins, especially A and D, has been proven to be very harmful. Provided a puppy is receiving a balanced diet, it is most unlikely there will be a deficiency, whereas hypervitaminosis (an excess of vitamins) has become quite common due to owners and breeders feeding unneeded supplements. The only time you should feed extra vitamins to your puppy is if your veterinarian advises you to.

Minerals

These provide strength to bone and cell tissue, as well as assist in many metabolic processes. Examples are calcium, phosphorous, copper, iron, magnesium, selenium, potassium, zinc, and sodium. The recommended amounts of all minerals in the diet has not been fully established. Calcium and phosphorous are known to be important, especially to puppies. They help in forming strong bones. As with vitamins, a mineral deficiency is most unlikely in pups given a good and varied diet. Again, an excess can create problems—this applying equally to calcium.

Water

This is the most important of all nutrients, as is easily shown by the fact that the adult dog is made up of about 60 percent water, the puppy containing an even higher percentage. Dogs must retain a water balance, which means that the total intake should be balanced by the total output. The intake comes either by direct input (the tap or its equivalent), plus water released when food is oxidized, known as metabolic water (remember that all foods contain the elements hydrogen and oxygen that recombine in the body to create water). A dog without adequate water will lose condition more rapidly than one depleted of food, a fact common to most animal species.

Curlies love a good romp in an open stream or lake, but they also need clean, fresh water for drinking at all times.

AMOUNT TO FEED

The best way to determine dietary requirements is by observing the puppy's general health and physical appearance. If he is well covered with flesh, shows good bone development and muscle, and is an active alert puppy, then his diet is fine. A puppy will consume about twice as much as an adult (of the same breed). You should ask the breeder of your puppy to show you the amounts fed to their pups and this will be a good starting point.

The puppy should eat his meal in about five to seven minutes. Any leftover food can be discarded or placed into the refrigerator until the next meal (but be sure it is thawed fully if your fridge is very cold).

Puppies and young Curlies will consume much more food than a full-grown adult will and you must adjust the meals accordingly. Consult your breeder or veterinarian.

If the puppy quickly devours its meal and is clearly still hungry, then you are not giving him enough food. If he eats readily but then begins to pick at it, or walks away leaving a quantity, then you are probably giving him too much food. Adjust this at the next meal and you will quickly begin to appreciate what the correct amount is. If, over a number of weeks, the pup starts to look fat, then he is obviously overeating; the reverse is true if he starts to look thin compared with others of the same breed.

WHEN TO FEED

It really does not matter what times of the day the puppy is fed, as long as he receives the needed quantity of food. Puppies from 8 weeks to 12 or 16 weeks need 3 or 4 meals a day. Older puppies and adult dogs should be fed twice a day. What is most important is that the feeding times are reasonably regular. They can be tailored to fit in with your own timetable—for example, 7 a.m. and 6 p.m. The dog will then expect his meals at these times each day. Keeping regular feeding times and feeding set amounts will help you monitor your puppy's or dog's health. If a dog that's normally enthusiastic about mealtimes and eats readily suddenly shows a lack of interest in food, you'll know something's not right.

Puppies between the ages of 8 to 16 weeks will need three or four meals a day. Once he is an adult, one or two meals will suffice.

TRAINING YOUR CURLY-COATED RETRIEVER

Once your puppy has settled into your home and responds to his name, then you can begin his basic training. Before giving advice on how you should go about doing this, two important points should be made. You should train the puppy in isolation of any potential distractions, and you should keep all lessons very short. It is essential that you have the full

When training a Curly puppy, you must have his full and undivided attention so that he will absorb your lessons faster and more completely.

attention of your puppy. This is not possible if there are other people about, or televisions and radios on, or other pets in the vicinity. Even when the pup has become a young adult, the maximum time you should allocate to a lesson is about 20 minutes. However, you can give the puppy more than one lesson a day, three being as many as are recommended, each well spaced apart.

Before beginning a lesson, always play a little game with the puppy so he is in an active state of mind and thus more receptive to the matter at hand. Likewise, always end a lesson with fun-time for the pup, and always—this is most important—end on a high note, praising the puppy. Let the lesson end when the pup has done as you require so he receives lots of fuss. This will really build his confidence.

COLLAR AND LEASH TRAINING

Training a puppy to his collar and leash is very easy. Place a collar on the puppy and, although he will initially try to bite at it, he will soon forget it, the more so if you play with him. You can leave the collar on for a few hours. Some people leave their dogs' collars on all of the time, others only when they are taking the dog out. If it is to be left on, purchase a narrow or round one so it does not mark the fur.

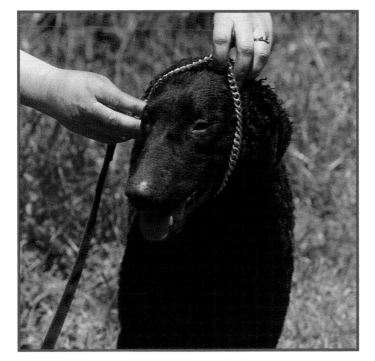

Using a training collar will assist you in teaching your Curly the proper commands.

Once the puppy ignores his collar, then you can attach the leash to it and let the puppy pull this along behind it for a few minutes. However, if the pup starts to chew at the leash, simply hold the leash but keep it slack and let the pup go where he wants. The idea is to let him get the feel of the leash, but not get in the habit of chewing it. Repeat this a couple of times a day for two days and the pup will get used to the leash without thinking that it will restrain him—which you will not have attempted to do yet.

Next, you can let the pup understand that the leash will restrict his movements. The first time he realizes this, he will pull and buck or just sit down. Immediately call the pup to you and give him lots of fuss. Never tug on the leash so the puppy is dragged along the floor, as this simply implants a negative thought in his mind.

THE COME COMMAND

Come is the most vital of all commands and especially so for the independently minded dog. To teach the puppy to come, let him reach the end of a long lead, then give the command and his name, gently pulling him toward you at the same time. As soon as he associates the word come with the action of moving toward you, pull only when he does not respond immediately. As he starts to come, move back to make him learn that he must come from a distance as well as when he is close to you. Soon you may be able to practice without a leash, but if he is slow to come or notably disobedient, go to him and pull him toward you, repeating the command. Never scold a dog during this exercise—or any other exercise. Remember the trick is that the puppy must want to come to you. For the very independent dog, hand signals may work better than verbal commands.

THE SIT COMMAND

As with most basic commands, your puppy will learn this one in just a few lessons. You can give the puppy two lessons a day on the sit command but he will make just as much progress with one 15-minute lesson each day. Some trainers will advise you that you should not proceed to other commands until the previous one has been learned really well. However, a bright young pup is quite capable of handling more than one command per lesson, and certainly per day. Indeed, as time progresses, you will be going through each command as a matter of routine before a new one is attempted. This is so the puppy always starts, as well as ends, a lesson on a high note, having successfully completed something.

Call the puppy to you and fuss over him. Place one hand on his hindquarters and the other under his upper chest. Say "Sit" in a pleasant (never harsh) voice. At the same time, push down his rear end and push up under his chest. Now lavish praise on the puppy. Repeat this a few times and your pet will get the idea. Once the puppy is in the sit position you will release your hands. At first he will tend to get up, so immediately repeat the exercise. The lesson will end when the pup is in the sit position. When the puppy understands the command, and does it right away, you can slowly move backwards so that you are a few feet away from him. If he attempts to come to you, simply place him back in the original position and start again. Do not attempt to keep the pup in the sit position for too long. At this age, even a few seconds is a long while and you do not want him to get bored with lessons before he has even begun them.

THE HEEL COMMAND

All dogs should be able to walk nicely on a leash without their owners being involved in a tug-of-war. The heel command will follow leash training. Heel training is best done where you have a wall to one side of you. This will restrict the puppy's lateral movements, so you only have to contend with forward and backward situations. A fence is an alternative, or you can do the lesson in the garage. Again, it is better to do the lesson in private, not on a public sidewalk where there will be many distractions.

With a puppy, there will be no need to use a choke collar as you can be just as effective with a regular

You and your Curly will benefit greatly by having him learn the sit command. These two guys know it well, which keeps them in the boat instead of gallivanting out on the lake!

one. The leash should be of good length, certainly not too short. You can adjust the space between you, the puppy, and the wall so your pet has only a small amount of room to move sideways. This being so, he will either hang back or pull ahead—the latter is the more desirable state as it indicates a bold pup who is not frightened of you.

Hold the leash in your right hand and pass it through your left. As the puppy moves ahead and strains on the leash, give the leash a quick jerk backwards with your left hand, at the same time saying "Heel." The position you want the pup to be in is such that his chest is level with, or just behind, an imaginary line from your knee. When the puppy is in this position, praise him and begin walking again, and the whole exercise will be repeated. Once the puppy begins to get the message, you can use your left hand to pat the side of your knee so the pup is encouraged to keep close to your side.

It is useful to suddenly do an about-turn when the pup understands the basics. The puppy will now be behind you, so you can pat your knee and say "Heel." As soon as the pup is in the correct position, give him lots of praise. The puppy will now be beginning to associate certain words with certain actions. Whenever he is not in the heel position he will experience displeasure as you jerk the leash, but when he comes alongside you he will receive praise. Given these two options, he will always prefer the latter—assuming he has no other reason to fear you, which would then create a dilemma in his mind.

Once the lesson has been well learned, then you can adjust your pace from a slow walk to a quick one and the puppy will come to adjust. The slow walk is always the more difficult for most puppies, as they are usually anxious to be on the move.

If you have no wall to walk against then things will be a little more difficult because the pup will tend to wander to his left. This means you need to give lateral jerks as well as bring the pup to your side. End the lesson when the pup is walking nicely beside you. Begin the lesson with a few sit commands (which he understands by now), so you're starting with success and praise. If your puppy is nervous on the leash, you should never drag him to your side as you may see so many other people do (who obviously didn't invest in a good book like you did!). If the pup sits down, call him to your side and give lots of praise. The pup must always come to you because he wants to. If he is dragged to your side he will see you doing the drag-ging—a big negative. When he races ahead he does not see you jerk the leash, so all he knows is that something restricted his movement and, once he was in a given position, you gave him lots of praise. This is using canine psychology to your advantage.

Always try to remember that if a dog must be disciplined, then try not to let him associate the discipline with you. This is not possible in all matters but, where it is, this is definitely to be preferred.

THE STAY COMMAND

This command follows from the sit. Face the puppy and say "Sit." Now step backwards, and as you do, say "Stay." Let the pup remain in the position for only a few seconds before calling him to you and giving lots of praise. Repeat this, but step further back. You do not need to shout at the puppy. Your pet is not deaf; in fact, his hearing is far better than yours. Speak just loudly enough for the pup to hear, yet use a firm voice. You can stretch the word to form a "sta-a-a-y." If the pup gets up and comes to you simply lift him up, place him back in the original position, and start again. As the pup comes to understand the command, you can move further and further back.

The next test is to walk away after placing the pup. This will mean your back is to him, which will tempt him to follow you. Keep an eye over your shoulder, and the minute the pup starts to move, spin around and, using a sterner voice, say either "Sit" or "Stay." If the pup has gotten quite close to you, then, again, return him to the original position.

As the weeks go by you can increase the length of time the pup is left in the stay position—but two to three minutes is quite long enough for a puppy. If your puppy drops into a lying position and is clearly more comfortable, there is nothing wrong with this. Like-wise, your pup will want to face the direction in which you walked off. Some trainers will insist that the dog faces the direction he was placed in, regardless of whether you move off on his blind side. I have never believed in this sort of obedience because it has no practical benefit.

THE DOWN COMMAND

From the puppy's viewpoint, the down command can be one of the more difficult ones to accept. This is because the position is one taken up by a submis-

Stay is another important command for your Curly to learn. Not only does it help him pose for nice pictures, but it also gives you an opportunity to keep him in check while you perform various tasks.

sive dog in a wild pack situation. A timid dog will roll over—a natural gesture of submission. A bolder pup will want to get up, and might back off, not feeling he should have to submit to this command. He will feel that he is under attack from you and about to be punished—which is what would be the position in his natural environment. Once he comes to understand this is not the case, he will accept this unnatural position without any problem.

You may notice that some dogs will sit very quickly, but will respond to the down command more slowly— it is their way of saying that they will obey the command, but under protest!

There are two ways to teach this command. One is, in my mind, more intimidating than the other, but it is up to you to decide which one works best for you. The first method is to stand in front of your puppy and bring him to the sit position, with his collar and leash on. Pass the leash under your left foot so that when you pull on it, the result is that the pup's neck is forced downwards. With your free left hand, push the pup's shoulders down while at the same time saying "Down." This is when a bold pup will instantly try to back off and wriggle in full protest. Hold the pup firmly by the

75

shoulders so he stays in the position for a second or two, then tell him what a good dog he is and give him lots of praise. Repeat this only a few times in a lesson because otherwise the puppy will get bored and upset over this command. End with an easy command that brings back the pup's confidence.

The second method, and the one I prefer, is done as follows: Stand in front of the pup and then tell him to sit. Now kneel down, which is immediately far less intimidating to the puppy than to have you towering above him. Take each of his front legs and pull them forward, at the same time saying "Down." Release the legs and quickly apply light pressure on the shoulders with your left hand. Then, as quickly, say "Good boy" and give lots of fuss. Repeat two or three times only. The pup will learn over a few lessons. Remember, this is a very submissive act on the pup's behalf, so there is no need to rush matters.

RECALL TO HEEL COMMAND

When your puppy is coming to the heel position from an off-leash situation—such as if he has been running free—he should do this in the correct manner. He should pass behind you and take up his position and then sit. To teach this command, have the pup in front of you in the sit position with his collar and leash on. Hold the leash in your right hand. Give him the command to heel, and pat your left knee. As the pup starts to move forward, use your right hand to guide him behind you. If need be you

The down position may be the most difficult for your Curly to learn because it is submissive. A bold puppy may want to challenge you, but once he learns who is the boss, he will comply easily.

Understanding "no" will make it easier for you to control your Curly and remind him of the rules. For instance, toys are okay, shoes aren't!

can hold his collar and walk the dog around the back of you to the desired position. You will need to repeat this a few times until the dog understands what is wanted.

When he has done this a number of times, you can try it without the collar and leash. If the pup comes up toward your left side, then bring him to the sit position in front of you, hold his collar and walk him around the back of you. He will eventually understand and automatically pass around your back each time. If the dog is already behind you when you recall him, then he should automatically come to your left side, which you will be patting with your hand.

THE NO COMMAND

This is a command that must be obeyed every time without fail. There are no halfway stages, he must be 100-percent reliable. Most delinquent dogs have never been taught this command; included in these are the jumpers, the barkers, and the biters. Were your puppy to approach a poisonous snake or any other potential danger, the no command, coupled with the recall, could save his life. You do not need to give a specific lesson for this command because it will crop up time and again in day-to-day life.

If the puppy is chewing a slipper, you should approach the pup, take hold of the slipper, and say "No" in a stern voice. If he jumps onto the furniture, lift him off and say "No" and place him gently on the floor. You must be consistent in the use of the command and apply it every time he is doing something you do not want him to do.

YOUR HEALTHY CURLY-COATED RETRIEVER

Dogs, like all other animals, are capable of contracting problems and diseases that, in most cases, are easily avoided by sound husbandry—meaning well-bred and well-cared-for animals are less prone to developing diseases and problems than are carelessly bred and neglected animals. Your knowledge of how to avoid problems is far more valuable than all of the books and advice on how to cure them. Respectively, the only person you should listen to about treatment is your vet. Veterinarians don't have all the answers, but at least they are trained to analyze and treat illnesses, and are aware of the full implications of treatments. This does not mean a few old remedies aren't good standbys when all else fails, but in most cases modern science provides the best treatments for disease.

Opposite: As a responsible Curly-Coated Retriever owner, you should have a basic understanding of the medical problems that affect the breed.

PHYSICAL EXAMS

Your puppy should receive regular physical examinations or check-ups. These come in two forms. One is obviously performed by your vet, and the other is a day-to-day procedure that should be done by you. Apart from the fact the exam will highlight any problem at an early stage, it is an excellent way of socializing the pup to being handled.

To do the physical exam yourself, start at the head and work your way around the body. You are looking for any sign of lesions, or any indication of parasites on the pup. The most common parasites are fleas and ticks.

Healthy teeth and gums are important to the overall well-being of your Curly. Check and brush his teeth regularly.

HEALTHY TEETH AND GUMS

Chewing is instinctual. Puppies chew so that their teeth and jaws grow strong and healthy as they develop. As the permanent teeth begin to emerge, it is painful and annoying to the puppy, and puppy owners must recognize that their new charges need something safe upon which to chew. Unfortunately, once the puppy's permanent teeth have emerged and settled solidly into the jaw, the chewing instinct does not fade. Adult dogs instinctively need to clean their teeth, massage their gums, and exercise their jaws through chewing.

It is necessary for your dog to have clean teeth. You should take your dog to the veterinarian at least once a year to have his teeth cleaned and to have his mouth examined for any sign of oral disease. Although dogs do not get cavities in the same way humans do, dogs'

The Hercules® by Nylabone® has raised dental tips that help fight plaque on your Curly-Coated Retriever's teeth and gums.

Curly-Coated Retrievers require some vegetable matter in their diet and the CarrotBone™(Made by Nylabone®) helps control plaque, eases the need to chew, and is nutritious.

teeth accumulate tartar, and more quickly than humans do! Veterinarians recommend brushing your dog's teeth daily. But who can find time to brush their dog's teeth daily? The accumulation of tartar and plaque on our dog's teeth when not removed can cause irritation and eventually erode the enamel and finally destroy the teeth. Advanced cases, while destroying the teeth, bring on gingivitis and periodontitis, two very serious conditions that can affect the dog's internal organs as well...to say nothing about bad breath!

Since everyone can't brush their dog's teeth daily or get to the veterinarian often enough for him to scale

the dog's teeth, providing the dog with something safe to chew on will help maintain oral hygeine. Chew devices from Nylabone® keep dogs' teeth clean, but they also provide an excellent resource for entertainment and relief of doggie tensions. Nylabone® products give your dog something to do for an hour or two every day and during that hour or two, your dog will be taking an active part in keeping his teeth and gums healthy…without even realizing it! That's invaluable to your dog, and valuable to you!

Nylabone® provides fun bones, challenging bones, and *safe* bones. It is an owner's responsibility to recognize safe chew toys from dangerous ones. Your dog will chew and devour anything you give him. Dogs must not be permitted to chew on items that they can break. Pieces of broken objects can do internal damage to a dog, besides ripping the dog's mouth. Cheap plastic or rubber toys can cause stoppage in the intestines; such stoppages are operable only if caught immediately.

The most obvious choices, in this case, may be the worst choice. Natural beef bones were not designed for chewing and cannot take too much pressure from the sides. Due to the abrasive nature of these bones, they should be offered most sparingly. Knuckle bones, though once very popular for dogs, can be easily

Nylabone® is the only plastic dog bone made of 100 percent virgin nylon, specially processed to create a tough, durable, completely safe bone.

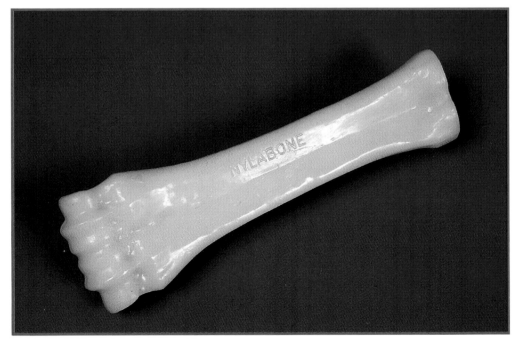

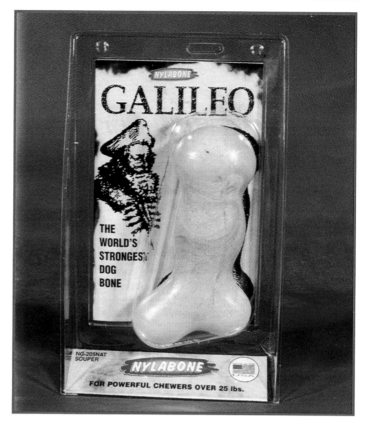

The Galileo™ is flavored to appeal to your Curly-Coated Retriever and is annealed so it has a relatively soft outer layer.

chewed up and eaten by dogs. At the very least, digestion is interrupted; at worst, the dog can choke or suffer from intestinal blockage.

When a dog chews hard on a Nylabone®, little bristle-like projections appear on the surface of the bone. These help to clean the dog's teeth and add to the gum-massaging. Given the chemistry of the nylon, the bristle can pass through the dog's intestinal tract without effect. Since nylon is inert, no microorganism can grow on it, and it can be washed in soap and water or sterilized in boiling water or in an autoclave.

For the sake of your dog, his teeth and your own peace of mind, provide your dog with Nylabones®. They have 100 variations from which to choose.

FIGHTING FLEAS

Fleas are very mobile and may be red, black, or brown in color. The adults suck the blood of the host, while the larvae feed on the feces of the adults, which is rich in blood. Flea "dirt" may be seen on the pup as very tiny clusters of blackish specks that look like freshly ground pepper. The eggs of fleas may be laid on the puppy, though they are more commonly laid off the host in a favorable place, such as the bedding. They normally hatch in 4 to 21 days, depending on the temperature, but they can survive for up to 18 months if temperature conditions are not favorable. The larvae are maggot-like and molt a couple of times before forming pupae, which can survive long periods until the temperature, or the vibration of a nearby host, causes them to emerge and jump on a host.

There are a number of effective treatments available, and you should discuss them with your veterinarian, then follow all instructions for the one you choose. Any treatment will involve a product for your puppy or dog and one for the environment, and will require diligence on your part to treat all areas and thoroughly clean your home and yard until the infestation is eradicated.

THE TROUBLE WITH TICKS

Ticks are arthropods of the spider family, which means they have eight legs (though the larvae have six). They bury their headparts into the host and gorge on its blood. They are easily seen as small grain-like creatures sticking out from the skin. They are often picked up when dogs play in fields, but may also arrive in your yard via wild animals—even birds—or stray cats and dogs. Some ticks are species-specific, others are more adaptable and will host on many species.

The cat flea is the most common flea of dogs. It starts feeding soon after it makes contact with the dog.

The deer tick is the most common carrier of Lyme disease. Photo courtesy of Virbac Laboratories, Inc., Fort Worth, Texas.

The most troublesome type of tick is the deer tick, which spreads the deadly Lyme disease that can cripple a dog (or a person). Deer ticks are tiny and very hard to detect. Often, by the time they're big enough to notice, they've been feeding on the dog for a few days—long enough to do their damage. Lyme disease was named for the area of the United States in which it was first detected—Lyme, Connecticut— but has now been diagnosed in almost all parts of the U.S. Your veterinarian can advise you of the danger to your dog(s) in your area, and may suggest your dog be vaccinated for Lyme. Always go over your dog with a fine-toothed flea comb when you come in from walking through any area that may harbor deer ticks, and if your dog is acting unusually sluggish or sore, seek veterinary advice.

Attempts to pull a tick free will invariably leave the headpart in the pup, where it will die and cause an infected wound or abscess. The best way to remove ticks is to dab a strong saline solution, iodine, or alcohol on them. This will numb them, causing them to loosen their hold, at which time they can be removed with forceps. The wound can then be cleaned and covered with an antiseptic ointment. If ticks are common in your area, consult with your vet for a suitable pesticide to be used in kennels, on bedding, and on the puppy or dog.

INSECTS AND OTHER OUTDOOR DANGERS

There are many biting insects, such as mosquitoes, that can cause discomfort to a puppy. Many diseases are transmitted by the males of these species.

A pup can easily get a grass seed or thorn lodged between his pads or in the folds of his ears. These may go unnoticed until an abscess forms.

This is where your daily check of the puppy or dog will do a world of good. If your puppy has been playing in long grass or places where there may be thorns, pine needles, wild animals, or parasites, the check-up is a wise precaution.

There are many parasites, such as fleas and ticks, in the great outdoors that your dog can encounter, so closely supervise him when he is outside.

SKIN DISORDERS

Apart from problems associated with lesions created by biting pests, a puppy may fall foul to a number of other skin disorders. Examples are ringworm, mange, and eczema. Ringworm is not caused by a worm, but is a fungal infection. It manifests itself as a sore-looking bald circle. If your puppy should have any form of bald patches, let your veterinarian check him over; a microscopic examination can confirm the condition. Many old remedies for ringworm exist, such as iodine, carbolic acid, formalin, and other tinctures, but modern drugs are superior.

Fungal infections can be very difficult to treat, and even more difficult to eradicate, because of the spores. These can withstand most treatments, other than burning, which is the best thing to do with bedding once the condition has been confirmed.

Mange is a general term that can be applied to many skin conditions where the hair falls out and a flaky crust develops and falls away.

Often, dogs will scratch themselves, and this invariably is worse than the original condition, for it opens lesions that are then subject to viral, fungal, or parasitic attack. The cause of the problem can be various species of mites. These either live on skin debris and the hair follicles, which they destroy, or they bury themselves just beneath the skin and feed on the tissue. Applying general remedies from pet stores is not recommended because it is essential to identify the type of mange before a specific treatment is effective.

Eczema is another non-specific term applied to many skin disorders. The condition can be brought about in many ways. Sunburn, chemicals, allergies to foods, drugs, pollens, and even stress can all produce a deterioration of the skin and coat. Given the range of causal factors, treatment can be difficult because the problem is one of identification. It is a case of taking each possibility at a time and trying to correctly diagnose the matter. If the cause is of a dietary nature then you must remove one item at a time in order to find out if the dog is allergic to a given food. It could, of course, be the lack of a nutrient that is the problem, so if the condition persists, you should consult your veterinarian.

INTERNAL DISORDERS

It cannot be overstressed that it is very foolish to attempt to diagnose an internal disorder without the advice of a veterinarian. Take a relatively common problem such as diarrhea. It might be caused by nothing more serious than the puppy hogging a lot of food or eating something that it has never previously eaten. Conversely, it could be the first indication of a potentially fatal disease. It's up to your veterinarian to make the correct diagnosis.

The following symptoms, especially if they accompany each other or are progressively added to earlier symptoms, mean you should visit the veterinarian right away:

Continual vomiting. All dogs vomit from time to time and this is not necessarily a sign of illness. They will eat grass to induce vomiting. It is a natural cleansing process common to many carnivores. However, continued vomiting is a clear sign of a problem. It may be a blockage in the pup's intestinal tract, it may be induced by worms, or it could be due to any number of diseases.

Diarrhea. This, too, may be nothing more than a temporary condition due to many factors. Even a change of home can induce diarrhea, because this often stresses the pup, and invariably there is some change in the diet. If it persists more than 48 hours then something is amiss. If blood is seen in the feces, waste no time at all in taking the dog to the vet.

Running eyes and/or nose. A pup might have a chill and this will cause the eyes and nose to weep. Again, this should quickly clear up if the puppy is placed in a warm environment and away from any drafts. If it does not, and especially if a mucous discharge is seen, then the pup has an illness that must be diagnosed.

Coughing. Prolonged coughing is a sign of a problem, usually of a respiratory nature.

Wheezing. If the pup has difficulty breathing and makes a wheezing sound when breathing, then something is wrong.

Cries when attempting to defecate or urinate. This might only be a minor problem due to the hard state of the feces, but it could be more serious, especially if the pup cries when urinating.

Cries when touched. Obviously, if you do not handle a puppy with care he might yelp. However, if he cries even when lifted gently, then he has an internal problem that becomes apparent when pressure is applied to a given area of the body. Clearly, this must be diagnosed.

Refuses food. Generally, puppies and dogs are greedy creatures when it comes to feeding time. Some might be more fussy, but none should refuse more than one meal. If they go for a number of hours without showing any interest in their food, then something is not as it should be.

General listlessness. All puppies have their off days when they do not seem their usual cheeky, mischievous selves. If this condition persists for more than two days then there is little doubt of a problem. They may not show any of the signs listed, other than perhaps a reduced interest in their food. There are many diseases that can develop internally without displaying obvious clinical signs. Blood, fecal, and other tests are needed in order to identify the disorder before it reaches an advanced state that may not be treatable.

WORMS

There are many species of worms, and a number of these live in the tissues of dogs and most other animals. Many create no problem at all, so you are not even aware they exist. Others can be tolerated in small levels, but become a major problem if they number more than a few. The most common types seen in dogs are roundworms and tapeworms. While roundworms are the greater problem, tapeworms require an intermediate host so are more easily eradicated.

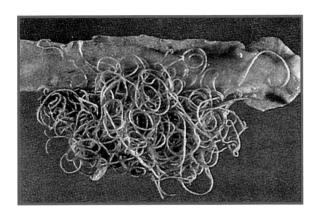

Roundworms are spaghetti-like worms that cause a pot-bellied appearance and dull coat, along with more severe symptoms, such as diarrhea and vomiting. Photo courtesy of Merck AgVet.

Roundworms of the species *Toxocara canis* infest the dog. They may grow to a length of 8 inches (20 cm) and look like strings of spaghetti. The worms feed on the digesting food in the pup's intestines. In chronic cases, the puppy will become pot-bellied, have diarrhea, and will vomit. Eventually, he will stop eating, having passed through the stage when he always seems hungry. The worms lay eggs in the puppy and these pass out in his feces. They are then either ingested by the pup, or they are eaten by mice, rats, or beetles. These may then be eaten by the puppy and the life cycle is complete.

Larval worms can migrate to the womb of a pregnant bitch, or to her mammary glands, and this is how they pass to the puppy. The pregnant bitch can be wormed, which will help. The pups can, and should,

Whipworms are hard to find unless you strain your dog's feces, and this is best left to a veterinarian. Pictured here are adult whipworms.

be wormed when they are about two weeks old. Repeat worming every 10 to 14 days and the parasites should be removed. Worms can be extremely dangerous to young puppies, so you should be sure the pup is wormed as a matter of routine.

Tapeworms can be seen as tiny rice-like eggs sticking to the puppy's or dog's anus. They are less destructive, but still undesirable. The eggs are eaten by mice, fleas, rabbits, and other animals that serve as intermediate hosts. They develop into a larval stage and the host must be eaten by the dog in order to complete the chain. Your vet will supply a suitable remedy if tapeworms are seen or suspected. There are other worms, such as hookworms and whipworms, that are also blood suckers. They will make a pup anemic, and blood might be seen in the feces, which can be examined by the vet to confirm their presence. Cleanliness in all matters is the best preventative measure for all worms.

Heartworm infestation in dogs is passed by mosquitoes but can be prevented by a monthly (or daily) treatment that is given orally. Talk to your vet about the risk of heartworm in your area.

BLOAT (GASTRIC DILATATION)

This condition has proved fatal in many dogs, especially large and deep-chested breeds, such as the Weimaraner and the Great Dane. However, any dog can get bloat. It is caused by swallowing air during exercise, food/water gulping or another strenuous task. As many believe, it is not the result of flatulence. The stomach of an affected dog twists, disallowing food and blood flow and resulting in harmful toxins being released into the bloodstream. Death can easily follow if the condition goes undetected.

The best preventative measure is not to feed large meals or exercise your puppy or dog immediately after he has eaten. Veterinarians recommend feeding three smaller meals per day in an elevated feeding rack, adding water to dry food to prevent gulping, and not offering water during mealtimes.

VACCINATIONS

Every puppy, purebred or mixed breed, should be vaccinated against the major canine diseases. These are distemper, leptospirosis, hepatitis, and canine parvovirus. Your puppy may have received a temporary vaccination against distemper before you purchased him, but be sure to ask the breeder to be sure.

The age at which vaccinations are given can vary, but will usually be when the pup is 8 to 12 weeks old. By this time any protection given to the pup by antibodies received from his mother via her initial milk feeds will be losing their strength.

Rely on your veterinarian for the most effectual vaccination schedule for your Curly-Coated Retriever puppy.

The puppy's immune system works on the basis that the white blood cells engulf and render harmless

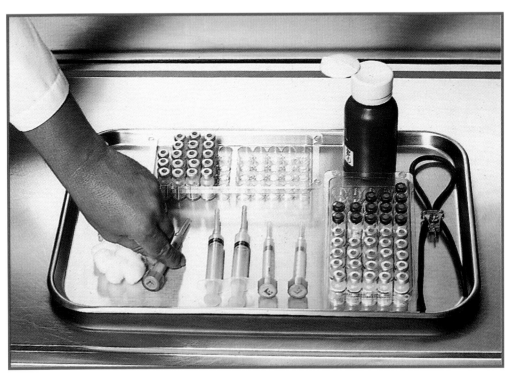

attacking bacteria. However, they must first recognize a potential enemy.

Vaccines are either dead bacteria or they are live, but in very small doses. Either type prompts the pup's defense system to attack them. When a large attack then comes (if it does), the immune system recognizes it and massive numbers of lymphocytes (white blood corpuscles) are mobilized to counter the attack. However, the ability of the cells to recognize these dangerous viruses can diminish over a period of time. It is therefore useful to provide annual reminders about the nature of the enemy. This is done by means of booster injections that keep the immune system on its alert. Immunization is not 100-percent guaranteed to be successful, but is very close. Certainly it is better than giving the puppy no protection.

Dogs are subject to other viral attacks, and if these are of a high-risk factor in your area, then your vet will suggest you have the puppy vaccinated against these as well.

Your puppy or dog should also be vaccinated against the deadly rabies virus. In fact, in many places it is illegal for your dog not to be vaccinated. This is to protect your dog, your family, and the rest of the animal population from this deadly virus that infects the nervous system and causes dementia and death.

ACCIDENTS

All puppies will get their share of bumps and bruises due to the rather energetic way they play. These will usually heal themselves over a few days. Small cuts should be bathed with a suitable disinfectant and then smeared with an antiseptic ointment. If a cut looks more serious, then stem the flow of blood with a towel or makeshift tourniquet and rush the pup to the veterinarian. Never apply so much pressure to the wound that it might restrict the flow of blood to the limb.

In the case of burns you should apply cold water or an ice pack to the surface. If the burn was due to a chemical, then this must be washed away with copious amounts of water. Apply petroleum jelly, or any vegetable oil, to the burn. Trim away the hair if need be. Wrap the dog in a blanket and rush him to the vet. The pup may go into shock, depending on the severity of the burn, and this will result in a lowered blood pressure, which is dangerous and the reason the pup must receive immediate veterinary attention.

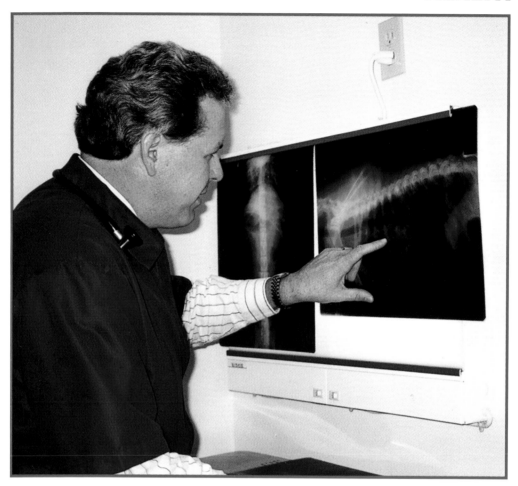

It is a good idea to x-ray the chest and abdomen on any dog hit by a car.

If a broken limb is suspected then try to keep the animal as still as possible. Wrap your pup or dog in a blanket to restrict movement and get him to the veterinarian as soon as possible. Do not move the dog's head so it is tilting backward, as this might result in blood entering the lungs.

Do not let your pup jump up and down from heights, as this can cause considerable shock to the joints. Like all youngsters, puppies do not know when enough is enough, so you must do all their thinking for them.

Provided you apply strict hygiene to all aspects of raising your puppy, and you make daily checks on his physical state, you have done as much as you can to safeguard him during his most vulnerable period. Routine visits to your veterinarian are also recommended, especially while the puppy is under one year of age. The vet may notice something that did not seem important to you.

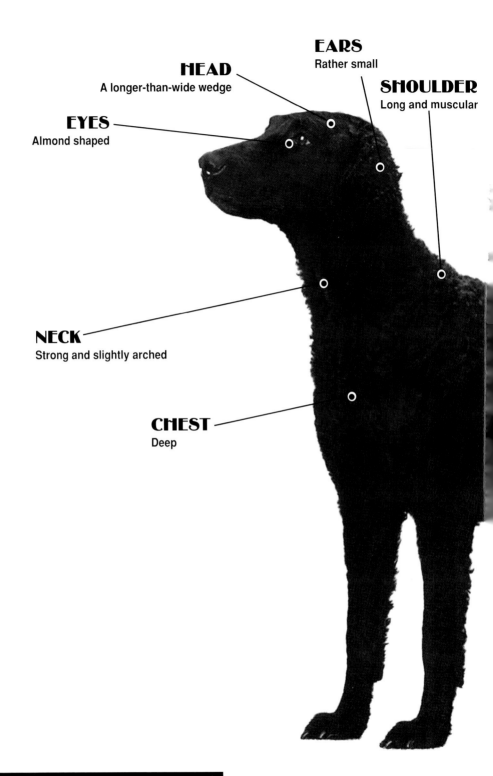

EARS
Rather small

HEAD
A longer-than-wide wedge

SHOULDER
Long and muscular

EYES
Almond shaped

NECK
Strong and slightly arched

CHEST
Deep

Westminster Kennel Club 1997 Best of Breed Ch. Ptarmigan Gale at Riverwatch, CD, owned by Gary E. and Mary Meek.